Mind As Builder

MIND AS BUILDER

The Positive-Mind Metaphysics of Edgar Cayce

Mitch Horowitz

bestselling author of *The Miracle Club*

Revised and Expanded

Published 2019 by Gildan Media LLC
aka G&D Media
www.GandDmedia.com

Front cover design by David Rheinhardt of Pyrographx

Interior design by Meghan Day Healey of Story Horse, LLC

Library of Congress Cataloging-in-Publication Data is available
upon request

ISBN: 978-1-7225-0268-3

10   9   8   7   6   5   4   3   2   1

*Dedicated to A.R.E. members,
past, present, and future.*

"... the spiritual is the *life*;
the mental is the *builder*;
the physical is the *result*."

—Edgar Cayce reading 254–42,
July 15, 1928

Contents

———◦•◦———

*   *   *

This book is based on a talk delivered at the Association for Research and Enlightenment (A.R.E.) on April 1, 2016, "Mind As Builder: Ancient Wisdom and Modern Insight."

Preface

———◦•◦———

When I visit A.R.E.'s headquarters in Virginia Beach, I always feel that I'm not only among friends, but also collaborators. Being there gives me an opportunity to focus and question some of my own ideas.

You'll have to put up with my repeating something that I've stated before about A.R.E. As Ronald Reagan once remarked, "If you have something you believe in deeply, it's worth repeating." I take that to heart.

As far as I'm concerned, A.R.E. is the greatest growth center our nation has produced. I've spoken and studied at spiritual centers on both coasts. But I find something truly special about A.R.E., not only because the institution and its staff and members exude the good will and neighborliness that was such a deep part of Edgar Cayce's character, but also because A.R.E. is the member-supported, nonsectarian growth center that Edgar and his son Hugh Lynn considered vitally necessary for the spiritual culture of this nation.

A.R.E. grew out of the most difficult period in Edgar Cayce's adult life. It was in the early 1930s, after his hospital in Virginia Beach had closed. The hospital, which now stands refurbished as a health spa and cafe, combined all opathic and alternative treatments with many of the ideas from Edgar's channeled medical readings. Its opening in 1929 represented the realization of a lifelong dream for Edgar. But its closure in February 1931, less than two years after it began, reflected not only an economic failure brought on by the Great Depression, but also Edgar's personal failure to navigate arguments and frictions among trustees and donors, who had abruptly pulled their support.

Had Edgar been a better and more engaged manager, he might have fostered a different outcome. He felt this sharply. "I've been tested," he told his wife Gertrude. "And I've failed."

With the closing of the hospital, there was no longer any real organization or congregation around

Edgar's work, beyond the daybed where he reclined for his readings, often given for strangers who lived long distances away, and the kitchen table where his transcriber Gladys Davis would sit with him and reply to correspondence. In early 1931, with the Great Depression grinding on and Virginia Beach emptied out for the winter, Edgar felt profoundly isolated.

Edgar had not only seen the dream of his hospital fail, but with it, he came to feel that he had wasted several earlier years of his life unsuccessfully wildcatting for oil in Texas in hopes of self-financing the now-shuttered facility. With broken relations and spent years behind him, he withdrew into reading Scripture, fishing, and chopping wood.

In June, Edgar's eldest son, Hugh Lynn Cayce, approached his father with an extraordinary idea. And I ask you to note this very carefully, because there was genius and power in what Hugh Lynn brought to his father. He said:

Maybe there's something wrong with us. Suppose we stop expecting people to do things for us and start doing them for ourselves. The world doesn't owe us a living because we have a psychic medium in the family; we ought to work for what we get just as everyone else does . . .

I think it would be wise if we stopped looking for large donations, stopped dreaming of another hospital, and concentrated on developing a little stock-in-trade. Then, when the next change comes, we'll be better prepared and we won't muff it . . .

I'll take over the job of manager of [A.R.E.]. We'll keep it small; we'll have a modest budget and a modest program.

We'll work quietly, by ourselves, with the help the local people who are interested. We'll start study groups. We'll take series of readings on various subjects. We'll build up a library on psychic phenomena . . .

Later in this book, we'll more fully examine the content and principles of Hugh Lynn's statement.* But for the moment, consider the main thrust of what he's saying, which is: We created a situation where we grew dependent on one or two wealthy donors; and when those relationships frayed, when we were left to our own devices, we could no longer

---

* For the complete account of Hugh Lynn's statement, see the appendix, "The Path Out of the Failure."

function. We need a radically different approach—we must do things ourselves, as best we're able. We need our own vehicle, our own newsletters, magazines, and research projects; and, most of all, our own network of members who don't just show up at the front door when they want a reading for one particular problem, or want to contact Aunt Bessie from beyond, and then vanish. But rather we need a membership base that takes a steady, concerted interest in metaphysical questions, in spiritual self-development, and in the teachings that come through the readings, including medical, past life, and spiritual. This membership should be counted on to maintain a lifelong commitment to these interests, and to the organization.

When I visit A.R.E. today, and I'm certain many of you feel this too, I walk the campus grounds, go through the buildings and library, as well as the new structures that have been added, and within the physicality of the place, I feel the sense that all of these things are an expression of that one idea that Hugh Lynn brought to his father—which is that the work must be sustained by the love and dedication of its students. There are many great spiritual centers in America; that's one way in which we're very fortunate. But I really don't think that any spiritual center has that kind of back story. This place was born on the basis of an idea. An idea is an extraordinary thing, but I must also add this: for an idea to work, it must be executed with assiduousness and dedication. Great ideas are great only in potential; they rely on great execution.

Spirit Is the Life

Our topic is, of course, the principle of "mind as builder." This is a foundational aspect of the Edgar Cayce teachings. In more than 600 of his channeled readings, Edgar used the phrase "the mind is the builder" or sometimes "the mental is the builder." In a reading he gave on July 15, 1928, probably one of the great days in this spiritual work, Edgar said from a trance state: "... the spiritual is the *life*; the mental is the *builder*; the physical is the *result.*" Now, isn't that what transpired in connection with Hugh Lynn's idea? Let's take apart Edgar's statement, using Hugh Lynn as an example.

Hugh Lynn understood that his father's work was good work, because it provided a window, a channel of sacred influence into the world, and opened up possibilities in the life of the individual. So, first of all, when dealing with the principle of "mind as builder," one must demonstrate a special kind of persistence and confidence, knowing that the object of one's desires is demonstrably sound. Where does that confidence come from?

A lot of people walk around acknowledging, "I'm insecure, I'm not confident." That outlook is so common that we see comedians and entertainers crafting a whole character or persona around the notion of being insecure. I'm thinking of Woody Allen, who is not actually insecure at all. He is an extraordinary artist and a powerful person; but he built his screen persona around the idea of being neurotic and second-guessing. We all recognize and laugh at some aspect of ourselves in that caricature. Generally speaking, people do have problems with confidence. But consider: If "the spiritual is the life"—then that principle contains the solution to a lack of confidence. Is the work that you want to bring into the world, whatever it may be, spiritually sound? Is it something that is going to create a circuit of generativity and productivity among other people? Will it make other people better?

Confidence comes from the willingness to be a vessel for something higher. That's why Hugh Lynn was authentically confident. Edgar, too, was confident about the nature of his work. Historically, Edgar has a reputation of being a humble, even retiring man. But as the scholar of religion, and one of my intellectual heroes, Harmon Bro, has noted, Edgar had a very decisive streak. Harmon spent time with Edgar toward the end of the seer's life, and wrote that Edgar stood "ten feet tall" and was "as strong-willed and capable of risks as Captain Ahab." When Edgar said no, he meant it. He didn't put on airs or behave obsequiously around the celebrities who occasionally approached him for readings. He added their names to the bottom of the wait list like everyone else. Vice President Henry Wallace, one of the most popular figures of the New Deal, was on that wait list when Edgar died in early 1945. Edgar didn't play favorites.

But let's not get hung up on the details. Being a vessel for something higher can mean all kinds of things. Almost every time I do an interview, whether it's on NPR or a New Age radio show, the host almost always harbors the assumption that somewhere in our discussion we're going to disparage *The Secret*. It sometimes seems like everybody hates *The Secret*—

that no ever liked it. I often encounter New Agers who engage in this game of punch-*The-Secret*. Now mind you, I call myself a New Ager, so I use that term in a positive way. To me New Age refers simply to therapeutic spirituality. I use the term with pride. But I do encounter New Age people who rush to disavow *The Secret,* as though doing so is a mark of seriousness. About twenty million people bought *The Secret,* yet I rarely find anyone who acknowledges it. Everyone feels compelled to participate in the backlash against it. People typically say things like: "The end of all spiritual work shouldn't be the manifestation of a Mercedes Benz." I can only smile when I hear that.

I've been in this work for a long time, writing and publishing books that analyze or express ideas from within the alternative spiritual culture. I have never once encountered anybody trying to manifest a Mercedes Benz. Rather, I encounter people dealing with addictions, marital problems, career issues, illness, trouble paying the rent—things that are as real as life gets. Never once have I met someone trying to manifest a shiny new car, or some such. But if it did happen, I would defend that person. Who am I to judge what creates value, productivity, and goodness in another person's life? I can easily imagine a situation where someone may have grown up in cir-cumstances in which his surroundings were ugly and depressing, and he simply wants the experience of being in touch with, or getting around in, what is simply a well-made car. That may not be all he wants, but it may represent something meaningful. I will never condemn that. Don't be too spiritually certain that the only things that matter are those we can't see. Test that. Verify that.

So, I don't want you to feel that when I'm talking about a sound influence, I'm restricting you to cer-tain parameters. But I do ask, above all, that you grapple with the question of whether this thing that you want to bring into the world is really going to *do good;* that is, can it become part of the circuitry or root system of good for another individual? Again, you don't have to let anybody dictate what that thing might be. No one should be made to feel that he is shallow, or somehow not "spiritual," if the thing he wants might be some kind of material gain or personal achievement. Money and resources do a lot of good. Money built the A.R.E.'s conference center. Money facilitated the devices you could be reading this book on, or the book you're holding in your hands right now. Money sends kids to school and helps bring beauty into the world. The Bible I read was financed by someone's contributions. So, please, let's not have restrictive attitudes toward money.

I was recently touched by the movie *Birdman* starring Michael Keaton. Seen from a certain perspective, the hero, played by Keaton, is a slightly over-the-hill movie star who is struggling to regain his past glory. But by the end, the film turns that conventional premise on its head. In fact, the protagonist seems like a fairly decent, sincere man who is in his natural element in the spotlight. It is right and worthy for him to be onstage—whereas those who criticize him seem less and less compelling. The movie asks you to take a second look at your values and to be certain that your ideas of right and wrong are authentic and not just handed-down truisms.

Let's return to Hugh Lynn, and what he told his father that day. He was filled with confidence, because he knew that his father was doing good work, and that view is, in a sense, widely held today. Some evangelical Christians feel strongly that Edgar Cayce was misled—I personally dispute that and believe we have a lot to talk over with our friends in the evangelical world. But suffice to say those who come near the Cayce work often agree that it gives people a broader sense of possibilities in healing, opens a new window on Scripture and other wisdom teachings, and facilitates forgiveness and reconciliation. A.R.E. and the Cayce centers and camps provide opportunities for kids, seniors, veterans, teachers, and all kinds of people from different backgrounds and religions. Edgar lived by the Gospels, and his work squares with Gospel ethics. Hugh Lynn knew that. His dependency was not on himself or his father, but on the fact that their work was in sync with a higher principle.

Hugh Lynn understood his father's words: "the spiritual is the life." Everything emanates from the higher, Hugh Lynn believed, and if you feel that you have placed yourself into the flow or channel of that emanation, you have good cause to feel confident.

Thoughts
Are Causative

The core phrase of Edgar's July 1928 reading is: "the mental is the builder." He later used the term "mind is the builder" or "mind as the builder." Again, this principle appeared in more than 600 readings, so the wording would differ here and there. But at this inceptive reading, he used the phrase "the mental is the builder."

What does it mean? It's a magnificent expression, and it was very suited to the times Edgar lived in. The late nineteenth and early twentieth centuries were a period of remarkable growth and influence for a distinctive American metaphysical culture, often known as New Thought. The American meta-physics of that era—which, in a sense, have become the American spirituality—rest on the principle that *thoughts are causative.*

Now, when looking at Edgar's language, I feel strongly that no one is just a passive or inert vessel for a certain message. The message that comes through you, or the thing that you live out, is marked by the times in which you live, the values you hold, and your background. So when Edgar was in a trance state, he would speak in tones and vocabulary that sounded a lot like the King James Bible. That was understandable, and even necessary, given who he was. Edgar was a Disciples of Christ Sunday school teacher. He read Scripture cover to cover for each year of his adult life. He regarded himself first and foremost as a Christian, and at times he struggled to understand some of the teachings that were coming through him, such as reincarnation, astrology, and numerology. These things are not commonly regarded as part of Christianity. I say "not commonly regarded" because one aspect of Edgar's brilliance was that he could, with great personal integrity, interpret parts of the Gospels to accommodate reincarnation and karma. Edgar studied Scripture and asked himself, in effect: "Can I understand, without playing games, whether these concepts fit into a Christian framework?" His answer was yes.

This is why I believe the individual channeler is more than just a loud speaker transmitting a message. Rather, a gifted channeler might be seen as a fine instrument, and a Stradivarius cello produces a different sound than a violin—or a harmonica for that matter. Most of the well-known channelers who have come up since Edgar first used and popularized the term "channel" sound very different from him. Helen Schucman, the Columbia University research psychologist and channeler who brought us *A Course in Miracles* in the 1960s and 70s, did not sound like Edgar at all. Schucman's contemporary, the poet Jane Roberts, who channeled the Seth material, sounded nothing like Helen Schucman. My friend Paul Selig, one of today's most significant channelers, doesn't sound like any of them.

Each channeler, like each individual, has outlooks, and reference points that stem from different times and situations, and that's going to affect how he or she sounds. I would hope that if what's being spoken is truth then there's a certain convergence in every channeler's work: a fundamental respect for the human search, a belief that each individual is sacred, and that doing violence to another individual—I'm not talking about defensive action but something that unjustly violates the sanctity of another—runs counter to the inner search.

I think we see that convergence. But, still, every channeler must function as part of his or her times. For that reason, I find it significant that in 1928, Edgar used the term "the mental is the builder." As I mentioned, America's spiritual culture at that time was ignited with the idea that *thoughts are causative*. That was a very American principle, and it remains at the heart of our culture today. That idea is the central tenet of the positive-thinking movement, and it undergirds our national life in ways that people don't always realize. Ronald Reagan was echoing this principle when he said "nothing is impossible," And likewise Barack Obama when he said, "Yes, we can."

Some people in journalism and academia today say, "I can't stand positive thinking. Get away from me with your refrigerator magnets and page-a-day calendars. That is for dupes." Yet even those who take that position innately echo the tenet that thoughts are causative. We all understand that self-disparaging attitudes are crippling, at least as much as foolish overconfidence, which is also crippling, as critics will point out. Both, of course, are attitudes of thought, self-conceptions—and both are impactful. This is just another way of affirming Edgar's statement.

Mesmerism

Decades before Edgar's birth, beginning roughly in the 1830s, America began developing an affinity for the idea of mental causation. The nation eventually became a springboard that projected the ideal of mental causation around the world. Various factors gave rise to this concept in American life. It was not conceived of in isolation, which nothing is. To cover all the historical bases, I would have to draw an arc from Hermetic Egypt to the Court of Louis XVI to Phil Donahue, which I do in my book *One Simple Idea*. And while I love tracing arcs on the family tree of ideas, we have limited time, and I don't want to make rushed connections. So let me restrict myself to modern events.

In Paris, shortly before the time of the French Revolution, there appeared a figure named Franz Anton Mesmer. He came from the German-speaking part of Switzerland. Mesmer was a physician, of a sort. He taught that an invisible, etheric fluid animates all of life—he called this fluid animal magnetism. Mesmer believed that if someone was suffering from some kind of physical or mental disorder, this animal magnetism was out of balance; Mesmer said that he could place people in trance states and while in these trance states manipulate their animal magnetism through various methods. He called these healing sessions séances, which is how that French term, loosely meaning "sittings," came into general use.

Mesmer didn't see himself as an occult figure. He saw himself as a rational figure, very much in line with the march of scientific progress. And, in a sense, he was. Because his brightest students later came to feel that Mesmer was not manipulating any kind of etheric fluid, but rather when he placed patients into a trance state he was influencing them by powers of suggestion. Mesmer and his students, in an era before psychological language, happened upon the first Western conception of what was later termed the subconscious mind. Mesmer's method came to be called hypnotism.

We routinely use terms such as séance, channeling, positive thinking, mesmerize, hypnotize, as if these things have always been with us—but they haven't. They are related to specific ideas and people. Mesmer was a catalyst for some of these ideas. And he was, not surprisingly, very controversial in his day; he had both powerful friends and enemies. People who were committed to democratic revolution in France tended to like Mesmer, because they felt that if all of humanity was animated by this invisible etheric fluid, then we are all just branches of the same tree, and there are no upper or lower classes. There's no aristocracy. In the same vein, some of Mesmer's students were early opponents of slavery. They argued that since Mesmer had proven that there is no essential difference among human beings, and that we're all shot through with this vitalizing invisible fluid or animal magnetism, what possible right does one person have to enslave another, to deprive that person of his physical freedom and human potential? If this invisible etheric fluid animates us all, civic equality must follow from that.

In late-eighteenth century France, nearly every advance in science and industry took on political overtones. The social and scientific ramifications of Mesmer's experiments were deadly serious. King Louis XVI was hostile to Mesmer, because the king's position depended upon the divine right of rule. Louis's divine rule did not comport with the notion that all of us are united by some kind of energy field. So Louis XVI assembled a commission of experts to critically study Mesmer. This was rather like the doctors who at one time stuck needles in Edgar Cayce's nail beds to test whether he was really in a trance state. The chair of Louis's royal committee was America's ambassador to France: Benjamin Franklin. The founding fathers had deep divisions of their own about Mesmer. Franklin and Thomas Jefferson were suspicious of him. Both men, Jefferson in particular, were leery of orthodox religion, and to them Mesmer smacked of a throwback to the days of soothsaying. Others viewed it differently. One of Mesmer's most dedicated students was the Marquis de Lafayette, the French hero of the American Revolutionary War, and a close friend of George Washington's. He even induced Mesmer and Washington to exchange letters.

Writing from France, Lafayette praised Mesmer in letters to Washington in 1784. "I know as much as any conjuror ever did . . ." he told Washington. "I will get leave to let you into the secret of Mesmer, which you may depend upon is a grand philosophical discovery." Lafayette was preparing to visit the new United States in fall of that year, not only to see Washington, but also to make a pilgrimage to the nation's first Shaker village outside of Albany, N.Y. Lafayette had heard about the Shakers entering trance states, holding séances, receiving communications from beyond, and he believed that these activities might correspond with Mesmer's theories. He wanted to investigate matters for himself.

A story began circulating in American historical literature in the early 1940s that shortly before Lafayette set sail for the U.S., he had an audience with King Louis XVI, and the King teased him for being friends with Mesmer, and wondered what Lafayette's friend General Washington would think of all this mumbo-jumbo. I got a kick out of this story, but I could not find the source—and I wondered whether it was really true. A historian always has to ask that question. People are constantly attributing things to Gandhi or Napoleon or William James that they never said. Was somebody walking behind Napoleon on the battlefield with a quill and leaf of paper writing things down while dodging cannon fire? And if Louis XVI really said this, who overheard it?

I searched and searched for the original quote and came up cold—but eventually I confirmed it. It turns out that following the French Revolution and Reign of Terror, a surviving French military officer who had spent years hanging around Louis XVI's court wrote a ten-volume series on court intrigues. Only the French would do this. I have a friend who is a professor of French history who helped me translate the pertinent passage. Sure enough there was Louis teasing Lafayette: "What will Washington think when he learns that you have become Mesmer's chief apothecary apprentice?" Lafayette was undeterred. He handed Washington a letter from Mesmer, in which the healer asked for Washington's support to open an American branch of his Society of Harmony, the organization that taught Mesmer's methods.

In a letter dated June 16, 1784, Mesmer told Washington: "It appeared to us that the man who merited most of his fellow men should be interested in the fate of every revolution which had for its object the good of humanity." When Mesmer compared his theories to a revolution, he was making a loaded point. The same French advocates of social reform who held an interest in Mesmerism had also found inspiration in the American Revolution. Mesmer was trying to place himself in league with democratic revolutions. And it wasn't entirely farfetched. Again, some saw what occurred in Mesmer's séance parlors as the first glimmer that there existed a deeper aspect of who we are as humans, something that defied rank or labels.

Until his death in 1815, Mesmer remained committed to his theory of animal magnetism. It often happens, however, that radical ideas must be refined and clarified by a future generation before becoming useful. Mesmer's best students believed that while the master had uncovered something essentially true, he was wrong about the existence of an etheric animal magnetism. As alluded earlier, they felt the teacher's methods actually revealed the presence of a deeper mind within us, something that lay beneath our rational faculties.

Consider how prescient this was. These experimenters were functioning in the 1780s, 1790s, and early 1800s. They possessed no psychological vocabulary. No one did. Westerners wouldn't begin to talk about a subconscious or unconscious mind until the late 1880s, when William James and his collaborators in psychical research began to speak of a "subliminal mind." That was the seed from which Sigmund Freud derived his theory of the unconscious. James's idea of the subconscious was broader than Freud's. James and his colleagues saw the subconscious mind somewhat like Mesmer's students did: an overarching and influential engine of thought that impacted physicality, individual agency, and—possibly—spanned beyond the faculties of the five senses.

Yet rather than growing, Mesmerism petered out in post-revolutionary France. During the Reign of Terror many of Mesmer's students were imprisoned or killed. Many of his critics met with the same fate. There was chaos. But a trickle of Mesmer's students came to the U.S. One became an instructor in French history at the military academy at West Point, N.Y. In 1812, he delivered the first public presentations of Mesmerism in America, giving rise to a new generation of Mesmerists. Like their European counterparts, American acolytes moved away from the master's reliance on animal magnetism. Among the homegrown experimenters was a Maine clockmaker named Phineas Quimby. It was Quimby who struck the initial note of the positive-mind revolution, which later resounded in Edgar Cayce's work.

New Thought

In 1833, Phineas Quimby was suffering from tuberculosis, for which there was no viable treatment.
American medicine throughout much of the nineteenth century was in a disastrous state. Medicine
was the one branch of science in which the New
World lagged behind Europe. European physicians
had inherited knowledge through a guild network
over the years. It wasn't much, but they did have
botanical remedies, could set a bone, and possessed
some ability to lessen suffering. On the whole, doctors in Europe were prosperous and well treated.
Few were tempted to make the dangerous journey
across the Atlantic.

As late as the early 1890s, it remained difficult to find talented physicians in America. It was rarer still to find doctors who could teach other physicians. For many years, the nation had just three teaching hospitals, in Boston, Philadelphia, and New York City. In the frontier states, many practicing physicians had no medical training at all beyond what they read in books. Their remedies could be medieval, like applying leeches. It was considered therapeutically useful to create "weeping wounds" and use bloodletting to promote bodily health. Physicians routinely used poisons, such as mercury, to cause excessive sweating, in another attempt at "draining" the body. Quimby was subjected to this treatment. The clockmaker had nowhere to turn. One day in 1833, he tried a remedy suggested by a friend. The ancient Greeks sometimes used rigorous horseback riding as a bodily tonic. One morning, Quimby embarked a wild buggy ride in the Maine countryside. He felt exuberant after his ride and reported sustained relief from tuberculosis symptoms. His "recovery," he observed, had nothing to do with the buggy ride but with the sense of emotional zeal it gave him. He reasoned that emotions play a significant role in health.

Quimby soon encountered itinerant Mesmerist lecturers who drew similar conclusions. He grew intrigued with the Mesmerist outlook that inner mental mechanisms impact physicality. Although Quimby belonged to no church or congregation, he developed a spiritual outlook about creative cosmic laws coursing through the body. In fact, Quimby's view was fairly close to what Edgar Cayce said nearly a century later: "the spiritual is the life." Quimby further believed that these spiritual laws enter our experience through the medium of thought: "mind is the builder," as Edgar said. Finally, these laws, in Quimby's view, create outer physicality: "the physical is the result."

In the years ahead, Quimby took on a dynamic student named Mary Glover Patterson. She later became known to history as Mary Baker Eddy, the founder of Christian Science. Following Quimby's death in early 1866, Mrs. Eddy made her own revelatory discovery, which she codified in her 1875 book *Science and Health,* the central statement of Christian Science. For well over a century, a debate has raged over whether Mrs. Eddy pilfered Quimby's ideas. I do not share that view. Mrs. Eddy and Quimby each had distinct thought systems. The differences are not such that anybody needed to be the bad guy.

Mrs. Eddy took a different view of the human mind than Quimby, and Edgar for that matter. She did not see the mind as a channel of divine energies. Rather, she saw the human mind as the seat of delusive ideas, violence, hatred, prejudice, and illness. She believed that matter itself was illusory—a false image of the mortal mind—and the only true reality was the Universal Mind of God. This led to her practice of eschewing "material medicines."

The Cayce readings differ. Edgar taught that the individual occupies, belongs to, and is influenced by various spheres of existence—including the material. He considered our material world very real. On January 27, 1935, Edgar gave a reading for an A.R.E. study group. One of his questioners seemed to ask about Christian Science: "Do you not believe if one can make herself positive to *only* the *good* she can overcome all physical ills of the body, without medicine, provided she feeds it right and treats it right?" Edgar responded: "What manner of body in a material world can live, survive or remain material without material sustenance? In each sphere of activity there are the attributes of same. The body-physical may indeed be healed without medicine, but it becomes rather the ethereal than material." (705–2) So while Edgar is saying that life is not exclusive to the material realm, for the time that we exist in it, we are subject to its laws. This is an important distinction to which I will return.

It is not always easy for people to appreciate what a radical metaphysic Mrs. Eddy was teaching. She was saying that we exist in a world of illusion: matter does not exist, evil and illness do not exist—these are figments of the mortal mind. But if "the doors of perception were cleansed," as William Blake put it, the mind of God could come through.

The other night I watched the movie *The Matrix* with my kids. Many of you know *The Matrix* in which human beings exist in a false, computer-generated world, and are in reality unconscious slaves. Every spiritual group says *"That's it, that's our idea!"* I'm not sure where the founding concept of the movie came from, but it has elements in common with the philosophy of Gurdjieff, Gnosticism, various Eastern teachings, and Christian Science. In any case, it's a brilliant work of art.

I was struck by a scene in which the hero, Neo, is sitting in his boss's office getting chewed out for something while outside the window appear these window washers using squeegees to clean the glass.

That, in a way, is Mrs. Eddy's philosophy. She taught that we do not have *perceptive* minds. The mortal mind promulgates only illusion and illness. There is only one real mind, the Mind of the Creator. When Jesus healed people during his ministry on earth that was the ever-operative Mind of God revealed. The illusory man-mind, Mrs. Eddy taught, must be dissolved so the Higher Mind can be revealed. Mrs. Eddy had her own bracingly original metaphysics. I consider her one of the true spiritual geniuses that our nation has produced.

A wide range of religious experimenters embraced, and sometimes remade, the ideas of both Quimby and Mrs. Eddy. As this was unfolding in the late nineteenth century, mainstream American medicine was undergoing radical changes. Perhaps the most seismic change came in 1893 with the opening of Johns Hopkins School of Medicine in Baltimore. Johns Hopkins was the first university-scale research hospital in the nation. The school imported teaching methods from Europe, including residencies and research requirements. It often surprises people that this occurred as late as 1893 when America was already on the threshold of becoming a super power. It took that long for the nation to advance beyond the abuses and lagging ideas of the nineteenth century.

Concurrent with progress in medicine, state legislatures began passing licensure laws that shut down the operations of many mental and prayer healers, people who were often offshoots of Quimby's and Mrs. Eddy's work. New laws prohibited alternative healers from advertising medical services. The philosopher William James, who is my true hero, spoke out against these licensure laws, because he felt that they would stifle experiments in the new mental therapeutics before their insights could be evaluated. James experimented with New Thought and Christian Science methods himself.

The philosopher protested that some professional medical associations were pushing for restrictive licensure laws less out of concern for public safety than the wish to corner the market for allopathic practitioners alone, who could advertise services, freely practice medicine across state lines, and be recognized as the sole legitimate wing of medicine. Himself a Harvard M. D., James detected a guild mentality among many traditional physicians, and believed them overeager to dismiss unconventional therapies.

This is not to suggest that alternative practitioners themselves didn't have serious problems. Some practitioners made sensationalized claims and charged for services they were incapable of delivering. But it wasn't compellingly clear that the field of alternative healing was endangering public health. James testified before the Massachusetts state legislature that nightmare scenarios were uncommon, and often drummed up by yellow journalism. Fatality rates among patients of alternative and traditional healers were not notably different.

James did support laws governing transparency in advertising. He believed that a healer should be required to disclose his degrees or credentials, and that the individual patient could thereafter make his decision.

James lost the battle. In state after state, licensure laws pushed many alternative practitioners from the market. Never one to depend on the winds of public opinion, Mrs. Eddy was quick to grasp the implications of the licensure movement. Christian Science practitioners were able to carve out some protection for themselves on constitutional grounds. Other healing movements withered.

Economic changes were also sweeping the American landscape. Commerce was booming. The stock market was growing, and the proliferation of stocks and bonds made it seem like money could appear from out of the ether. For the first time in American history, a majority of people were no longer earning their living on farms but relocating and working for companies in big towns and cities. Railroads were connecting those towns. Department stores were opening around the country The Sears catalogue was being shipped into households nationwide. Cutlery, kitchenware, mass-produced furniture, and trinkets you could put up in your cabinet were suddenly within reach of everyday people.

Americans wanted a piece of the action. Some of the practitioners inspired by Mrs. Eddy and Quimby began to broaden their conceptions of the powers of the mind from healing to material gain. As the new century dawned, Americans encountered popular books like *The Science of Getting Rich* by social reformer Wallace D. Wattles, and *The Conquest of Poverty* by feminist and labor reporter Helen Wilmans. In 1898, a suffragist named Elizabeth Towne started a popular New Thought magazine called *Nautilus*. Towne, Wattles, and Wilmans, and many of their contemporaries were united in the conviction that the new mental metaphysics, varyingly called New Thought, Divine Science, Science of Mind, and Unity, could not only heal the body but also the wallet, and could help you attain every conception of success.

But what most historians miss is that these new mind-power practitioners weren't just prosperity peddlers. Like Mesmer, they saw their movement as part of the march of social progress—they advocated for voting rights, anti-lynching legislation, the rights of immigrants and women, and inveighed against child labor and sweatshops. Many called themselves socialists. Wattles ran for office on the ticket of the Socialist Party, and Towne became the first female alderman of Holyoke, Massachusetts. The new generation believed that mind-power could work hand in hand with other reformist movements to bring about a world of prosperity, education, and solidarity. They believed mind metaphysics were among the tools a person could use to erase, or at least ease, class, gender, and racial lines.

Many Americans were ready to listen. They filled New Thought churches. They formed New Thought clubs, prayer circles, schools, and seminaries. They grew connected through magazines, newspapers, and mail-order correspondence courses and ministries. New Thought teachers understood how to rally a constituency. There's nothing wrong with that. The life's blood of any thought movement is its audience. Jesus didn't sit by himself somewhere staring at the ground; he spoke on a mountaintop.

The American way was to reach a broad audience—and the people came.

Some social critics, from H. L. Mencken to Barbara Ehrenreich, have regarded New Thought followers, then and now, as dupes and sheep. They are wrong. They simply did not understand the movement they were judging. In surviving letters, articles, journals, and diaries, people speak of having some of the most meaningful experiences of their lives studying New Thought, or reading a book like Helen Wilmans' *The Conquest of Poverty*.

Wilmans led an extraordinary career. Her life was a New Thought parable of liberation. She was a newspaper reporter in Chicago in the early 1880s—one of the pioneering female reporters of that era. Everything had gone against her in life. She was fired from jobs, divorced from her husband, left to raise daughters on her own, and lived one step ahead of eviction from her Chicago boarding house. More than anything, Wilmans wanted to start her own labor newspaper. She wanted to bring the ideas of mind-power to working people. One day in 1882, she asked her Chicago editor if he would invest in the venture. He dismissed the idea out of hand. In despondency, Wilmans left the newspaper offices and wandered through the streets of Chicago on a dark November afternoon. She thought to herself: I am completely alone; there is no one on whom I can depend. But as those words sounded in her head, she was filled with a sense of confidence. It occurred to her that she didn't *have* to depend on anyone else—she could depend on the power of her mind. This was the New Thought gospel. "I walked those icy streets like a school boy just released from restraint," Wilmans wrote. "My years fell from me as completely as if death turned my spirit loose in Paradise."

Wilmans returned to her boarding house, and her landlord asked why she was home before the work day ended. She told him she had lost her job and exuberantly described plans for a newspaper; he was so taken that he floated her rent and financially backed her first issue. That year, Wilmans began publishing *The Woman's World*, which became a voice for both women's independence and New Thought. In future years, she spun it into a New Thought publishing house and mail-order company. For a time, Wilmans may have been the most influential female religious figure in the country next to Mrs. Eddy, even though her name is not remembered.

Wilmans met with a tragic end. In the 1890s, she grew quickly rich. She remarried and relocated to

Seabreeze, Florida, to open a metaphysical university. In Florida, she became a successful real estate developer in the Daytona Beach area. Some local real estate big shots didn't want this woman coming in, buying up tracts of land, and infringing on their territory. So they used political connections to persuade the postmaster general in 1901 to investigate Wilmans' mail-order house, from which she also sold prayer treatments. The postmaster general accused her of pedaling humbuggery, and banned her from using the mails. Wilmans could no longer sell her books, magazines, treatments, or even reach her followers.

She fought the government's fraud charges and won. A circuit-court judge threw out the government's case in 1905, and scolded prosecutors for attempting to drag Wilmans' metaphysical beliefs before the bench. In one of my favorite lines in judicial history, the judge said: "The court is not a society for psychical research."

But none of it mattered. Legal bills had drained her finances. Her second husband soon died. She attempted to launch a new magazine in 1906, but despite her court victory, the postmaster general, in an unconscionable act, flouted the court's ruling and refused to lift its ban. Her opponents had choked off her air supply. Depressed and alone, Wilmans died in 1907.

Wilmans was a giant—and her audience loved her. But she was harassed out of existence. I'm proud to be dedicating one of my new books to her.

What I'm trying to demonstrate with these stories is that no historian or academic can broadly claim, not to me, that this was all just a bunch of American gullibility and nonsense. There is no historical validity, and none today, to the premise that New Thought and mental therapeutics are a national con job. There is no soundness to the claim that figures like Mrs. Eddy, Helen Wilmans, Wallace D. Wattles, or others, were grifters shearing sheep. That wasn't the history of Christian Science or New Thought. I can argue for that in either historical or metaphysical terms. I care about both.

During the Great Depression, New Thought provided a tremendous lifeline to people, as I believe it does today. Books like *Think and Grow Rich* and *How to Win Friends and Influence People*, which were published in the 1930s, weren't offering false hopes; they were offering concrete ideas. How do you behave in the workplace? What is the way to accomplish things inside of a large organization? How do you foster the necessary comity with coworkers? A lot of Americans found themselves for the first time working in sales jobs or in large offices. They didn't always know what constituted professional behavior. A book like *How to Win Friends and Influence People* taught them—and I say with dead seriousness that I wish people in the twenty-first century would read that book again, because with the advent of social media we need to relearn its lessons.

A tone of viciousness permeates many online comments, texts, and even emails. It is deteriorative to our culture. Young people in office settings often do not understand that an email is not a social media posting, to which you can respond or not based on whether you feel like it. Exchanging email is like talking with someone face to face, and if you ignore a reasonable email, it's the equivalent of standing in front of someone without acknowledging him, which engenders bewilderment and hostility. We shouldn't be so sophisticated as to think that we no longer need or never did need, books like *How to Win Friends and Influence People*. We desperately need such books.

Physical Is the Result

The history of mind metaphysics is more than just history. It is a body of living ideas that has affected people in this country for generations. The mental metaphysics of New Thought and Edgar Cayce have opened new possibilities and ways of life. That's been true for me, as I write about in my book *One Simple Idea*; that continues to be true for many people today.

Once you hear Edgar's phrase, "mind is builder," you never forget it. There's a certain solidity to it. It summarizes both a universal truth and the new metaphysics that were sweeping the Western world when Edgar first uttered it. Edgar followed it by saying "the physical is the result." Mesmer and Quimby drew a direct connection between the faculties of thought and physical wellness. Mrs. Eddy, by contrast, believed that physical health resulted from the individual becoming a cleansed door of perception. Mrs. Eddy would have agreed with the makers of *The Matrix*. She shared their conception of humanity trapped in an illusory world, where no tactile experience is real. Hence, she would have disputed Edgar's contention that we exist in both spiritual and material realms and are governed by the laws of both. My own sympathies are with Edgar, and I'll try to explain why.

When Edgar said, "the physical is the result," his statement, first of all, must be interpreted broadly. He's talking about health—but not health alone. He also would have applied that statement to the buildings that make up A.R.E.'s campus, and soon. Hugh Lynn had an idea about starting a self-reliant, member-supported organization. His idea translated to other people who provide the skills, resources, and membership necessary for A.R.E. to function. Edgar clarified in various readings that ideas do, in fact, translate to physical forces. So, I ask myself, and each of you: How do we relate to the physical? This is an area ripe for experiment within New Thought philosophy. It's the most important question for me right now. I'm struggling with it, and I invite you to struggle with me.

For me, the most brilliant teacher in the New Thought tradition is Neville Goddard, a British Barbadian born in 1905. He taught in America for most of his life and died in 1972. This is a man I truly love; he is one of the most influential figures in my own search. Neville maintained that not only is mind the builder, but the mind conceals an ultimate truth whose dimensions we do not grasp. Neville taught that the human imagination is the God of Scripture, and that Scripture is not a work of history but rather a parabolic reenactment or allegory of man's inner development. Inner development, in Neville's view, involves awakening to the idea that thought is the creator of all, is God. Scripture is a symbolic retelling of the truth that you are God clothed in human flesh.

Neville meant this in the most literal sense. Hence, he would say that these words you're hearing or reading do not belong to me—they are yours. They are a product of your readiness to hear them, as everything is a product, ultimately, of your emotive and mental states. When I read Neville, it's like I get drunk on "spiritual wine." The Shakers once used that expression to describe "spiritual gifts" that gave them pleasures, they said, that went beyond anything physically conceived. Neville argued for his thesis with exquisite persuasiveness and simplicity. No matter how many times he restated his ideas, they sounded as though he was saying or writing them for the first time.

If you haven't experienced Neville's essays or lectures, I urge you to consider them. I recently narrated an audio edition of Neville's first book called *At Your Command*, which includes my essay "Neville Goddard: A Cosmic Philosopher," in which I talk further about his ideas and how they relate to quantum theory. I challenge anyone reading or hearing these words to experience one of Neville's books or lectures, and not feel that you haven't just encountered something extraordinary. And yet the man himself never once used a fifty-cent word. If you really know what you are talking about, you ought to be able to speak simply.

So, if I love Neville, and if I'm so persuaded by his convictions, why then do I also agree with Edgar that we necessarily experience physical limitations? This is the core challenge that we face today in the New Thought movement, a movement of which I consider myself apart, and a movement that is close in nature to A.R.E. Some of us believe, as Neville does, that all of life results from one great mental super law. Some people call it the Law of Attraction, but whatever term you use, some seekers consider this ever-operative, over arching mental super law as the ultimate truth of life.

I think—and I am really struggling with this—that that is possibly true, that we do live under one ultimate mental law. As we'll see, we receive hints of that possibility in certain quantum physics experiments, where objects are affected by the decisions of the researcher to measure or not measure something. Quantum experiments have now been going on for about eighty years, and anybody who thinks that he understands, or can proscribe, the implications of those experiments, understands nothing. We'll return to this later. Now, I said that I think it's possible that we do live under the ultimate law of mind. But I also think that we are not necessarily able to experience that truth in the manner of existence that we occupy.

You could talk about the law of gravity, for example, as being an ultimate truth, and so it is. For a law to be a law, it must be consistent; it must be ever-operative. But the way that you experience gravity on earth differs from how you would experience gravity on the moon or in the vacuum of space or on Jupiter. The same law is always going on, it's real, and it's there. But I'm incapable of experiencing this law on earth in the way that an astronaut experiences it on the moon. And that begs the question of whether we live under multiple laws and forces, rather than a law of mentality. My answer is, yes, of course we live under multiple forces. Gravity is always going on, nobody questions that. But mass is also going on, so if you are on Jupiter, which is far more massive than earth, you experience a much greater pull of gravity. If you were physically on Jupiter, the gravity would crush you; you would be unable to move. The same law occurs on the moon, where you would be much lighter. You could jump ten feet in the air and hit a golf ball more than two miles, because the moon has less mass and, hence, less gravitational pull. The point is: I don't have to argue whether gravity is there; it evidently is there. But it operates differently in different realms of existence and circumstance. We may be experiencing something similar with the creative law of the mind.

Our bodies physically decay; mortality is a fact. There's been no exception to that, ever, including in the lives of saints and Christ himself. New Thought teacher Joseph Murphy, who died in 1981, would sometimes attempt to explain the mind's inability to affect mortality by saying that life is necessarily educative, and it must end so that other cycles may begin; and, in any case, he said, life would grow unbearably stagnant if immortality existed. That's true enough, but it's also a way of changing the subject. Physical decay is a fact, all lived experience dictates as much. That doesn't mean that Neville is necessarily wrong in his statement that mind is God, and that thought rules the universe. But I do think that even if the mind is a creative force, even perhaps the ultimate force, there coexist circumstances and matters of reality with which we must live, at least from our vantage point. We aren't God. Neville often quotes Jesus saying, "I and my Father are one, but my Father is greater than I." If Neville were here, and I wish he were, and maybe in some way he is, he would probably agree that the branch and the tree are the same thing, but they *experience different circumstances*, and the wind can blow down a branch but cannot blow down the tree. We aren't God.

I believe that Edgar was expressing something similar when he said it's insufficient to conclude that we live under the one-and-only influence of mind. We do have physical lives. But the extraordinary thing is that we've been granted the ability to question and to experiment with how, whether, or to what degree the mind serves as a medium of influence over the physical. That is the challenge of our generation. And we are living through an extraordinary period of revelations pertaining to that challenge.

Everything that I have noted about Edgar Cayce's views of the mind would come across as alien to most physicians and scientists who are working with placebo studies, or in quantum physics, or in a new field like neuroplasticity—yet these same researchers are simultaneously affirming them. In the field of neuroplasticity, researchers have demonstrated through brain scans that thoughts actually alter the neural pathways of the brain. Researchers are finding that holding a sustained thought eventually alters brain chemistry. For fifteen to twenty years, brain scans have shown that a program of successfully redirected thoughts change the actual pathways through which electrical impulses travel in your brain; the cellular gray matter itself is altered. This is as provable through brain scans as any other aspect of physical experience. It cuts against everything we heard growing up—it is literally mind over matter.

Edgar said, "the mind is the builder, the physical is the result"—that is the philosophical underpinning of the field of neuroplasticity. One of the most dynamic researchers in the field is clinical psychiatrist Jeffrey M. Schwartz, who works at UCLA with sufferers of Obsessive-Compulsive Disorder (OCD). Schwartz describes the mind as possessing a "directed mental force," with measurable physical effects. He found that if people with OCD followed a protocol of consistently redirecting their intrusive thoughts, not only would they experience relief from some of the ritualistic impulses of OCD, but physical changes would occur in the gray matter of their brains. The mind, he noted, wields a *"physical force"*—the emphasis is his. This runs contrary to what he learned coming up in his career as an M. D., and are search psychiatrist, but there it is.

Now, some scientists reject any kind of conversation along these lines. If I approach most medical researchers and ask, "Have you heard of Edgar Cayce?"—well, you can imagine the answer. But this isn't true of everyone. A scientist named Ted Kaptchuk heads up the program in placebo studies at Harvard Medical School. Now I want to be very careful, because when I bring up the name

Harvard Medical School, it's a lot like people quoting Napoleon and Gandhi who some supposes aid everything. People always claim to have heard about a Harvard Medical School report that proves whatever you like. Fiber's good for you; fiber's bad for you. Positive thoughts are good for you; positive thoughts are bad for you, and soon. I try to be careful when I make references to Harvard and not to quote from any study or finding without having read the primary sources.

Now, Kaptchuk is an intrepid thinker, and we're fortunate to have someone like him running a major center for placebo studies. In December of 2010, he and his colleagues published a study that you may have heard about: it's colloquially called the "honest placebo" study. They took a group of patients suffering from Irritable Bowel Syndrome (IBS) and gave them a sugar pill and told them, in effect: "You know what's in here? Nothing!" The researchers were entirely transparent, letting the subjects know that they were receiving an inert substance. This is the first time this was done in a placebo study. And even though the patients understood the facts, a significant number still reported substantial and sustained relief from this so-called honest placebo.

Consider that you are told that you are being given nothing—but still feel better. Everyone has his own pet theories as to why the study produced those kinds of results. But the Harvard researchers, to their credit, chose not to interpret their results. They said that what they were seeing was remarkable and warrants further research. We need more positions like that in public life. We need more questions and fewer certainties. The Harvard team was willing to hold a question, and I thought that was beautiful.

I'll say this much about the implications of the honest placebo experiment, and a possible area for further study. Many physicians are understandably wary of triggering the placebo response. Because by their nature, placebos require misleading the patient, however good the intent. But if we can find a way to transparently stimulate the same kind of hopeful expectancy that patients experience in placebo trials—and hopeful expectancy is presumably what triggers the placebo response, if there's any at all—it opens a whole new set of possibilities in mind-body medicine, and the therapeutic harnessing of mind and mood. What methods can be used to transparently induce these apparently restorative, healing moods?

Harvard's program in placebo studies produced another important paper in January 2013—and, again, I encourage you to look up these things for yourself; I don't want anyone to feel that I'm playing it fast-and-loose with clinical studies, which somehow magically seem to support my point of view. The 2013 study demonstrated that migraine sufferers experienced a greater degree of relief from their medication if the researcher or administering physician spoke in favor of the prescription. This too was a first: We generally measure the placebo effect by comparing an inert substance to an active medication, but here the researchers considered whether the placebo response could improve the efficacy of an already active medicine. The answer they found was yes. If your doctor or caregiver gives you "positive information" about a drug, and if you are told in a convincing manner and have no reason to doubt it, that encouragement, it seems, will net a greater improvement in your sense of recovery from taking the drug. We have no precise ways of measuring pain; it's an individual sensation. We measure pain by asking patients how they feel. Patients are asked to rank what they're feeling on a scale. Migraine sufferers in this study were given a certain protocol and experienced greater benefits if they were reassured of the efficacy of their prescription. So the placebo response, it seems, is perpetual—it impacts the tenor of our experience all the time.

Now, a French hypnotherapist named Emile Coué had the same insight in the early 1900s. You may not have heard of Coué, but you've probably heard of his confidence-building mantra, "Day by day, in every way, I'm getting better and better." What serious person could possibly believe that you could be helped by something like that? Well, the Harvard study validated one of Coué's core insights. Coué got on the scent trail of the therapeutic uses of the mind following an experience he had working as a pharmacist in northwestern France in the early twentieth century. He discovered, quite on his own, that when he spoke in favor of a formula that he was dispensing, his patients seemed to do better with it.

So, I'm reading this Harvard study and saying to myself, "Wow, more than a century ago, Coué had the same insight as the Harvard researchers." I decided to try a little experiment of my own and see if any of the members of the Harvard team had heard of Coué. I reached out to the scientist on the study team who was designated to speak to the press and other inquirers. He never got back to me. So I reached out to the program director Kaptchuk, who also worked on the study, and not only did he get back to me, but he said, "Of course I know about Coué"—and he quoted his day-by-day mantra. Kaptchuk said that they were not thinking of Coué when devising the experiment, but he agreed that it could comport with Coué's insights.

Do We See Reality?

We are living in an era in which certain insights that were known to some of our ancestors in the New Age, and to Edgar Cayce, are being rediscovered and validated by science.

UCLA's Jeffrey Schwartz feels that there should be a dialogue today between medical researchers who are working on neuroplasticity and physicists who are working in quantum physics. "The implications of direct neuroplasticity combined with quantum physics," he writes, "cast new light on the question of humanity's place, and role, in nature." I would add to that statement that there are also grounds for a conversation between physicists and serious students of metaphysics.

The question of the mind's influence is debated within quantum physics in what is called the "quantum measurement problem." In the quantum physics lab, the presence and position of a subatomic particle changes based upon the presence and decisions of the observer to take a measurement or not. Particles exist in a state of "superposition," or a wave state, in which they exist as potentialities, until a measurement is made. In this state of superposition, subatomic particles occupy multiple places at once. We know this because scientists can detect interference patterns. So if you were to fire a subatomic particle at two boxes, so to speak, it is provable that the particle occupied both boxes at the same time. The particle is localized in one box only after someone takes a measurement.

Again, we've been raised to believe that this cannot be right. In our world view, stuff is supposed to be in one place, not infinite places. A vase of flowers is here, not here *and* there. Well, quantum physics suggests that a thing *is* here and there—and if a law requires consistency, then the behavior of material in the particle lab must also be happening in our macro, day-to-day lives. But why don't we see it?

A physicist writing recently in *Scientific American* proposed a theory called "information leakage."

He noted that if you are observing something with very fine instrumentation, you are receiving all kinds of information, and discovering all kinds of detail, but all that gets lost when you pan back. As the microscope or measuring instrument moves backwards, the data received grows coarser, less reliable, less detailed. This writer theorized that maybe what we consider surreal in the particle world is really what's going on all the time, everywhere. But our five senses are coarse instruments, and we glean only a fraction of what's happening.

People think they are broaching these questions for the first time, but William James made the same proposition in 1902, in a series of lectures that became his book *The Varieties of Religious Experience.* James wondered if the mystic might be like a kind of microscope; he might see the details of reality more finely. The closer and closer you zoom in with a microscope, James wrote, the more information you receive. And the further and further you move back, the more information gets lost. If you take an image and copy it by some means, and you then copy it over and over again, that image will start to lose resolution. These facts may hint at why we do not see the same things in our macro world that are occurring all the time in the sub-atomic world.

And maybe, just maybe, things that happen in the macro world also hinge on our decisions, like the quantum researcher whose decision to measure or not measure, and whose vantage point when doing so, determines what will be there. Now there's something to experiment with. Neville Goddard provides the closest New Thought analog to this way of thinking. Experiment with his methods.

It's unfortunate that we face the same problem today that William James did during the licensure movement in the early 1890s, which is that we suffer a guild mentality in which few people are willing to open the doors of their work to discussion and consideration with people from other fields, so that we can glean as many insights as possible. Ted Kaptchuk at Harvard knows who Emile Coué is, and demonstrates that you can be interested in, or at least aware of, metaphysical thought and can also conduct research at the highest levels. Each pursuit can inform the other.

The laboratory that we in the metaphysical culture work in is our own experience. And that is very important. Some scientists dismiss "anecdote" or testimony. But testimony, when amassed over the course of years, amounts to something. This is why I love the classic literature of positive thinking. I love this literature not only for its insights into human nature but also for its total practicality. Researchers should take a second look at these books (or a first look as the case may be), because the popular literature of positive-mind metaphysics evinced an early instinct for topics that we are now exploring in clinical circles. Everyone who I have mentioned, from Helen Wilmans to Emile Coué to Neville Goddard to Edgar Cayce expressed certain insights that are clinically validated today. That isn't true of everything they said, but what confluence does exist is a starting point. You and I should be using their methods to continue the experiment in our own lives.

Day by Day: Exercises

———⚬✦⚬———

Here are three exercises for you to try on your own.

Exercise I: Stronger Every Day

I mentioned that contemporary researchers have validated one of Emile Coué's insights about hopeful expectancy. And there's another case where Coué's work is supported by current research. Just as Edgar Cayce's readings indicated, Coué noted that your mind is in an exquisitely suggestible state during the moments just before you drift off to sleep at night and just as you come to consciousness in the morning. Sleep researchers call this the "hypnagogic state." During this time, Coué recommended using his key mantra: "Day by day, in every way, I am getting better and better."

He specifically devised this mantra to be general, so that it would meet with little or no resistance from the rational mind. He prescribed repeating it in a gentle whisper, almost like you are praying, and saying it twenty times just before you nod off at night and twenty times just as you wake in the morning. He recommended getting a little string and knotting it twenty times and using it to count off your repetitions, almost as though you are saying a Rosary. Or you can just count on your fingers, whichever is easier.

And there's a still-further dimension to our minds during this time. Although it goes beyond the scope of my subject to go fully into this now, I care deeply about ESP research. There was a great ESP researcher named Charles Honorton who died at age 46 in 1992. In the 1980s, Honorton conducted a series of experiments called the ganzfeld experiments. Ganzfeld is German for "open field." Honorton hypothesized that if you could induce the hypnagogic state in people during their normal waking hours, usually by placing them in conditions of comfortable sensory deprivation where sound and light are muted, it might heighten the psychical powers of the mind, whose existence he hypothesized.

Honorton conducted tens of thousands of trials to measure this—people just have no idea how hard the authentic parapsychologist works, and how lonely, rigorous, and painstaking his field is. Honorton would take two subjects and place one in an isolation room, maybe in a reclining chair, wearing an eyeshade to block all light and headphones emitting white noise. The setting induced a relaxed, sensory-deprived state. You can see one of these isolation rooms at the Rhine Research Center in Durham, North Carolina, which continues the work of another of my heroes, researcher J. B. Rhine, who popularized the term ESP. Honorton and Rhine worked together for a time.

Honorton would then situate the other participant outside the isolation room. The second subject would attempt to mentally "send" an image to the isolated person. Using a meta-analysis of tens of thousands of trials, his own and those of others, Honorton found a consistently higher-than-chance rate of receivership during this state of mental relaxation. I write further about this in my *One Simple Idea*. Like Coué and Cayce, Honorton found that something mentally distinctive occurs during hypnagogia.

Shortly before his death, Honorton co-authored a journal article with one of his most ardent critics, Ray Hyman, who is a psychology professor at the University of Oregon and a skeptic of ESP research. In their paper, the two men agreed that the ganzfeld research was sound—the data was unpolluted. They further agreed that additional research is in order. That's all. Hyman did not change his mind—he maintained that the ESP thesis is wrong; but he agreed that Honorton's data, and that of other ganzfeld researchers in the1980s, was uncorrupt and the numbers presented an anomaly. Now that's authentic skepticism. My challenge to critics is this: It is unnecessary to pre-suppose that ESP exists. Rather, let's ask: Why is this statistical anomaly showing up? Can't we study it, as Honorton and Hyman suggested? If the data is unpolluted, then why are we getting these numbers? My problem with most ESP critics today is not that they want to have a debate and win—that's fine. Rather, they want no debate, and that leaves us intellectually impoverished.

Exercise II: The Three-Step Miracle

This exercise is based on a little book called *It Works*. I've personally given away more than a hundred copies of this book. It's a pamphlet written in 1926 by a Chicago type writer salesman. He didn't put his name on it. He used only his initials: R. H. J. His name was Roy Herbert Jarrett. He was a wonderful man, and he waited until he was well into middle age to produce this 28-page pamphlet. He wanted to be certain that he had validated his ideas in his own experience before making them public. Here is what I call the Three-Step Miracle. It's very simple. So simple that serious people are apt not to try it at all, because they think it seems silly. You try it and see.

The *first step* is to make a list of what you really want out of life. But not just any list, not some hokey list—not "I want to be happy." Rather, your list must result from mature, sustained scrutiny of your inner most desires. Things may appear on your list that make you uncomfortable. "I'm a nice person," you may tell yourself, blanching at some item. "I don't want to do this." Hold nothing back. Ethics can—and must—be brought in; your ideals must be generative. But for now, keep writing and rewriting this list with stark honesty. I can't emphasis enough not to rely on your mental habits, because we repeat things to ourselves all the time by rote, like "I like my job," "I want to travel," "I like this or that." No. Don't rely on anything rote. Don't rely on anything that you habitually tell yourself. Sit down and ask what you really want.

Your *second step* is to read the list morning, midday, and night. I advise following the hypnagogic method: Read it just when you are coming to in the morning. Read it at midday in a state of relaxation—perhaps after lunch when you experience mild drowsiness, and preferably someplace private. And, finally, read it just before you drift off to sleep at night. Carry the list with you. Read it other times as well. Think about it always.

Finally, *step three:* Tell no one what you are doing; it's your business, nobody else's. It's like the movie *Fight Club:* "You DO NOT talk about Fight Club!" If you tell other people, you are going to meet someone who will run down what you're doing or shake your resolve. We all have family members and friends who are hostile or jealous. You can spend your whole life asking why, but it's simply a fact, and you don't want anyone detracting from your sense of purpose. This exercise and your aims belong to you alone. Remain silent.

Then watch what happens—and express thanks when good things come to you. Demonstrate faith and gratitude. That's it. Try it. It's natural to hear something like this and say, "Can I get my money back?" It's natural to feel that way; what I'm prescribing seems too simple. Just try it. Then decide.

I believe that tremendous energies, and I say that broadly, become available to us when we come to terms with our deepest desires. But we rarely do so. We lazily believe we already know what we want—if you ask someone he will say, "Of course I know: I want this job, this apartment, to go on vacation at this place, and yes I want good things for my kids, and so on and so forth." That voice is not necessarily ours. There is another voice that we rarely discover, because we are self-conditioned by what we are supposed to want. This experiment, provided it's done with all your guts and all your being, will put you in front of ideas and aims that you may have never known you had.

Exercise III: A Definite Chief Aim

Napoleon Hill, the author of *Think and Grow Rich,* had a key idea that relates to what I just described. In fact, I'm dedicating an entire book to Hill's principle. Hill believed that in life you must have a definite chief aim. We waste and squander our energies, because we lack a definite aim. He felt strongly that if you don't have a definite chief aim—and Edgar talks in a similar vein about having an ideal—you go nowhere.

Hill did not mean a mere desire, but an all-consuming, passionately held drive. He said that most of us go through life with an admixture of competing aims, some of which directly contradict each another, such as wanting to be a leader while also wanting lots of leisure time. But people who succeed in some dramatic way, whether in the arts or business or some other pursuit, tend to structure their lives around one non-negotiable, passionately felt aim.

The natural response to that is: "But I want lots of things. And what about the list Horowitz told me to make . . . ?" Don't worry; it's fine to want lots of things. What I'm saying is that you must possess one non-negotiable, over-arching aim on which, next to the imperatives of health and home, you stake your existence. And, let me tell you, it may not be very romantic. The Gilded Age industrialist Andrew Carnegie said his aim was to get rich making steel. That may not set your heart on fire, but it's what he wanted. On a greater scale, Gandhi wanted to free a nation. It didn't mean that Gandhi didn't want a place to lay his head at night, or to be at peace, but his chief aim was to free a nation. Don't be embarrassed. It could be something that you think sounds petty or selfish. But, then, says who? Hugh Lynn Cayce's chief aim was to preserve his father's work at a self-supporting spiritual center, a place that did not have to seek anyone's permission to do anything. Well, A.R.E. now exists. What is your chief aim?

Approach this with deadly seriousness. Read Napoleon Hill's *Think and Grow Rich,* and read it like your life depends on it. The whole book is a study in the importance of having a definite aim. And remember, it can be any ethical aim—it doesn't have to be growing rich. He called the book *Think and Grow Rich* because the title hits people where they live and grabs their attention. Everyone with a heartfelt aim—every artist, activist, teacher, and soldier—should read his book. It is ultimately about how to translate an aim into reality. Whatever your goal or values, read the thing inside and out. I recommend rereading it every year.

I'm going to add one last exercise for extra credit. I assure you, you'll enjoy it. We are always told that change begins from within, and that is true. But there are methods of enlisting your inner energies that come from the outside. Within the limits of reason, I want you to dress however you want for the next week—and see what happens. I'm not suggesting that you attend a funeral in flip-flops, or that you do something that embarrasses or compromises people who depend on you. But you should feel at liberty to cultivate an outer appearance completely of your choosing. If you want to dress like a drum majorette, then dress like a drum majorette. The point is, if you can permit yourself to comport yourself however you want, you will find that it engenders in you a kind of confidence that abets your ability to get things done, and attracts people to you.

Previous generations were told, "Don't dress for the job you have, dress for the job you want" or "dress for success." Then along came Mark Zuckerberg with his hoody. I like his style; I'm convinced he's going to enslave us all someday, but he looks good. A rock critic once said that he went to work every day in the same brand of black suit and black t-shirt—it prepared him for anything. Steve Jobs wore New Balance sneakers, jeans, and the exact same style of black turtleneck for much of his adult life. He considered it a uniform; it made him feel relaxed and kept him from getting distracted with the morning decision of what to wear. Jobs believed that the world and its devices should be rendered accessible to each individual. That was reflected in how he approached his own choices.

These kinds of little things, which we may tell ourselves are "unspiritual" or unbefitting a serious person, can actually make a real difference by helping summon and vitalize some of mental and emotional energies we have been exploring. So just consider this a little extra credit assignment. Perhaps next time I'm at A. R. E, Kevin Todeschi, the CEO, will ask me why everyone is now coming to work in volleyball clothing, but so be it.

All that we've been considering is part of the wonderful gift given to us by Edgar Cayce. He encapsulated the philosophy of mental metaphysics in his beautiful statement from the reading of July 15, 1928: ". . . the spiritual is the life; the mental is the builder; the physical is the result." I ask that you take that teaching, and everything we've considered, and go and experiment, so that the next generation can look back on us in the same way that we look back on Edgar and Hugh Lynn.

What will you build in your life as an individual that will allow you to step back and say, "There, it's done; and it's good?" How will what you build contribute to the productivity and experience of another individual? And can what you've built be carried on—will it continue to be useful in years ahead? I wish you the deepest success in this undertaking. Now go and build.

Appendix I:
The Path Out of Failure

The closure—and rebirth—of the Cayce health center holds universal lessons in how to overcome setback.

In the winter of 1931, the Christian mystic and medical clairvoyant Edgar Cayce came to feel that his life's work had amounted to nothing.

Edgar had long dreamed of establishing a hospital based on his channeled health readings. But in February, the mystic's Virginia Beach hospital and research center ran out of operating money and was forced to close its doors, less than two years after opening. Patients had to leave, files were carted off, and Edgar wandered the halls alone gathering his personal belongings before the building was shuttered.

The financial collapse arrived after longtime contributors quarreled with Edgar and abruptly abandoned him and his work. The Great Depression did the rest to gut his 30-bed facility.

"I've been tested," Edgar told his wife Gertrude. "And I've failed."

Today, the original hospital building is not only back in the hands of the organization that Edgar founded, the Association for Research and Enlightenment (A.R.E.), but has recently undergone a major remodeling and is now a bustling facility that houses a school of massage, a refurbished health spa, new classrooms, the offices of a reconstituted Atlantic University, and a health-food restaurant that ranks with dining experiences in "crunchy capitals" like San Francisco and Boulder, Colo.

Edgar's dream of a dedicated health center is now alive in ways that he wouldn't have imagined back in the winter of 1931. How did this turnaround occur?

Months after the hospital's closing, while Edgar remained withdrawn and depressed, his eldest son, Hugh Lynn Cayce, then twenty-four, approached him with an idea to reconstitute the Cayce work. As the future A.R.E. director saw it, his father needed to free himself from dependency on one or two big donors, as well as from fly-by-night seekers strictly interested in a personal reading. Instead, Hugh Lynn envisioned a member-supported organization that would keep people involved in all facets of his father's work—spiritual growth, personal healing, and ancient mysteries—while also providing a steady base of member support.

In essence, Hugh Lynn called for self-determination. He wanted the newly formed A.R.E. to demonstrate: 1) financial independence, with a scrappy willingness to do as much, or as little, a sits member-based budget permitted; and 2) intellectual integrity, with a determination to organize, verify, and cross-reference the readings so that patients and seekers were not treated in isolation. Hugh Lynn's formula transformed temporary defeat into renewed action and purpose.

Hugh Lynn's program is every bit as serviceable for anyone facing setbacks today as it was for his father intheearly1930s. Here is what Hugh Lynn told Edgar, as recounted by Cayce family friend and biographer Thomas Sugrue:

"Maybe there's something wrong with us. Suppose we stop expecting people to do things for us and start doing them for ourselves. The world doesn't owe us a living because we have a psychic medium in the family; we ought to work for what we get just as everyone else does.

"In the first place, we don't know anything about the thing we're trying to sell. We look at the information as if it were a faucet. Just turn the tap and whatever we want flows out. We were going to give the world our wisdom—the wisdom that came out of the faucet when we turned the tap. We figured it was our wisdom because we had the faucet.

"We don't know anything about psychic phenomena. We have our own experiences, but we don't know what else has been done in the field.

"What do we know about the Life Readings? Do we know the history well enough to check the periods mentioned for people and give them a bibliography—a list of books and articles—with each reading? Certainly not!

"Do we know enough about philosophy, metaphysics, and comparative religion to check the readings on what is said in these fields?

"When a reading makes a statement and says it is a philosophical truth, do we know what philosophers believed the same thing, and what religions have it in their dogma?

"When a statement about anatomy, or about a disease, or about the use of a medicine or herb is made, do we know whether medical authorities believe the same thing or condemn it, or know nothing of the matter?

"If a person asked us for everything the readings have said about appendicitis, or ulcers of the stomach, or migraine, or the common cold, or epilepsy, or marriage, or forgiveness of sin, or love, could we produce it? Certainly not. That work was barely begun when the hospital closed. "I think it would be wise if we stopped looking for large donations, stopped dreaming of another hospital, and concentrated on developing a little stock-in-trade. Then, when the next change comes, we'll be better prepared and we won't muff it."

"I don't know how to do that sort of work—" Edgar began.

"You don't have to," Hugh Lynn said. *"I'll do it . . . I'll take over the job of manager of the*

Association. We'll keep it small; we'll have a modest budget and a modest program.

"We'll work quietly, by ourselves, with the help of the local people who are interested. We'll start study groups. We'll take series of readings on various subjects. We'll build up a library on psychic phenomena. "Then when people come and ask what we do, we can say something other than that we take two readings a day, send them to people who pay for them, and put copies in our files. That isn't much for an organization that goes around under the name of the Association for Research and Enlightenment."

I ask you to consider how Hugh Lynn's ideas can be applied in your own life today. I find four principles in his statement:

1. *Self-Sufficiency.* As much as possible, cultivate a sense of realistic self-reliance. Are your plans or projects rightly scaled, or are they overly dependent upon the resources or approval of others? Outsiders can withdraw their support just as quickly as they give it. Build on solid foundations.

2. *Higher Vision*. Regularly check yourself to be certain that your plans are based on the ethical and spiritual certainty of serving something higher, and interjecting real benefit into the world.

3. *Steady Goes It*. Build your projects patiently and methodically. Be willing to do as much, or as little, as resources permit. This is not only practical but also grants you the satisfaction of knowing that you are functioning without damaging compromises and within your own means.

4. *Sweat Equity*. Constantly ask: Am I performing my work with the highest quality and integrity? Do I suffuse my work with the skill and effort necessary to provide the finest possible service?

And, finally, I challenge you to apply these principles in one more way. If you are not already an A.R.E. member, please consider supporting the vision that Hugh Lynn brought into the world. With each of us who steps up, Hugh Lynn and Edgar's work is further validated and realized.

(This article originally appeared on the A.R.E. blog, April 18, 2016)

Appendix II:
Rediscovering Edgar

Who was Edgar Cayce, the day-to-day person?
Recently, I came a bit closer to gaining a feeling in my heart for Edgar the man when I was given the privilege of reintroducing and narrating a new audio and print edition of Thomas Sugrue's classic biography, *There Is a River*, jointly published by A.R.E. Press and TarcherPerigee.

I spent four days in a small recording booth narrating the full text of Sugrue's 1942 book, along with my new introduction. *There Is a River* was the only biography of Edgar published during his lifetime, and the book attracted national attention and established him as the best-known psychic of the twentieth century.

My involvement with the book helped me see Edgar less as a headline-making "miracle worker" than as exactly the person he said he was: a devout Christian, a deeply loyal man of agrarian roots, and a seeker who never knew quite how to understand his psychical gift, yet who determined that his trance readings would either serve the higher good or he would cease them altogether.

Edgar's self-perception informed Sugrue's title, from Psalms 46:4: "There is a river, the streams where of shall make glad the city of God ..." The seer regarded himself simply as a "channel"—a term he was among the first to use—of the Divine flow.

When encountering *There Is a River,* some readers are taken aback, as I first was, by its degree of family detail. Sugrue dedicates long passages to the marriages and living arrangements of various cousins, in-laws, aunts, and uncles. But I came to realize that this detail grew directly out of Edgar's literary choices, and the author's close proximity to him.

Sugrue spent several years in the late 1930s and early 1940s convalescing with Edgar in Virginia Beach. The journalist suffered from a debilitating joint disease and credited Edgar's readings with prolonging his life. During afternoons together, the men would talk for hours. Sugrue set the general framework of their discussions and augmented them with his own research and interviews. But it was Edgar who directed his biographer to the topics that mattered most to him.

There Is a River could not have been written any other way. For all Edgar's reputation as a "simple" man, he set his own priorities with an iron determination. Scholar Harmon Bro, who also spent time close to the seer, noted that Edgar stood "ten feet tall" and was "as strong-willed and capable of risks as Captain Ahab in Moby Dick." Edgar, while gentlemanly, deferred to no-one. He could be overheard on the phone telling Hollywood celebrities who wanted a reading that their names would be added to the wait list like everyone else's. (Even Franklin Roosevelt's vice president, Henry A. Wallace, a well-known seeker in mystical realms, sat on Edgar's wait list, never receiving his session by the time of Edgar's death in early 1945.)

Sugrue also devotes many pages to the details of Edgar's medical readings. These parts of the book amass an important record: First, they capture the primary thrust of Edgar's career as a healer, and, second, they demonstrate how hard his patients had to work on their own recoveries. Those who got better, Sugrue writes, were often those who followed Edgar's meticulous treatments as closely as possible. This was not easy. Communication was slow between the healer and his patients, who often lived far away; there was no Baar Products (today's supplier of Cayce remedies) or A.R.E. catalog from which to order materials; physicians were often hostile to the readings and would not assist; and the treatments could consume major parts of a patient's day.

For all the focus on family and medical matters, Sugrue also maps out a coherent and compelling spiritual vision behind Edgar's readings. In short, Sugrue finds that the teachings contain a definite theology: Men and women enter this earthly plane from prior incarnations and are charged with balancing out karmic influences from past lives; eventually—sometimes following many lifetimes of trial, error, and resolution—they rejoin the source of Creation. At the foundation of this cosmic theology is a deep sense of Christian ethics. It has Christ at its epicenter. But Edgar's theology also provides perhaps the nearest expression we have of a universal faith—one that unites and harmonizes the insights of the major religions, a topic I explore further in my introduction.

Another detail struck me with special poignancy—and it may be why Edgar's name has remained widely known. After Edgar's hospital closed, while he reeled from sorrow and watched key donors depart, the seer received a renewed sense of purpose from his eldest son, Hugh Lynn. Hugh Lynn Cayce hit upon a new idea of how the work should be carried out. "Maybe there's something wrong with us," he told his father in 1931. "Suppose we stop expecting people to do things for us and start doing for ourselves. The world doesn't owe us a living because we have a psychic medium in the family; we ought to work for what we get just as everyone else does."

Hugh Lynn proposed a radical new structure for the nascent Association for Research and Enlightenment. The organization would be member-supported—no more reliance on one or two fickle donors. And members would be motivated to remain involved in order to benefit from the association's educational resources and services. As Hugh Lynn saw it, A.R.E. would categorize the readings by topic and ailment; assemble a world-class psychical library; publish journals, newsletters, and books; and host conferences and programs. A.R.E. would fulfill its aim of "research and enlightenment"—all of it self-supported by people who felt a shared stake in the organization's mission.

This was one of the turning points of Edgar's life. Hugh Lynn's vision left its mark on A.R.E. and generations of members. The currents of the river did not end with the seer, but now flow through the ongoing reach of his work.

(This article originally appeared on the A.R.E. blog, July 2, 2015)

Appendix III:
Edgar Cayce: Ordinary Man, Extraordinary Messenger

The year 1910 marked a turning point in Western spirituality. It saw the deaths of some of the most luminous religious thinkers of the nineteenth century, including psychologist-seeker William James; popular medium Andrew Jackson Davis; and Christian Science founder Mary Baker Eddy. These three figures deeply impacted the movements in positive thinking, prayer healing, and psychical research.

Their death that year was accompanied by the rise to prominence of a new religious innovator—a figure who built upon the spiritual experiments of the nineteenth century to shape the New Age culture of the dawning era.* In autumn of 1910, *The New York Times* brought the first major national attention to the name of Edgar Cayce, a young man who later became known as the "father of holistic medicine" and the founding voice of alternative spirituality.

The Sunday *Times* of October 9, 1910, profiled the Christian mystic and medical clairvoyant in an extensive article and photo spread: *Illiterate Man Becomes a Doctor When Hypnotized*. At the time, Cayce (pronounced "Casey"), then thirty-three, was struggling to make his way as a commercial photographer in his hometown of Hopkinsville, Kentucky, while delivering daily trance-based medical "readings" in which he would diagnose and prescribe natural cures for the illnesses of people he had never met.

Cayce's method was to recline on a sofa or daybed; loosen his tie, belt, cuffs, and shoelaces; and enter a sleeplike trance; then, given only the name and location of a subject, the "sleeping prophet" was said to gain insight into the person's body and psy-

---

* The term "New Age" is often used to denote trendy or fickle spiritual tastes. I do not share in that usage: I use New Age to reference the eclectic culture of therapeutic and experimental spirituality that emerged in the late twentieth century.

chology. By the time of his death in January 1945, Cayce had amassed a record of more than 14,300 clairvoyant readings for people across the nation, with many of the sessions captured by stenographer Gladys Davis.

In the 1920s, Cayce's trance readings expanded beyond medicine (which nonetheless remained at the core of his work) to include "life readings," in which he explored a person's inner conflicts and needs. In these sessions, Cayce employed references to astrology, karma, reincarnation, and number symbolism. Other times, he expounded on global prophecies, climate or geological changes, and the lost history of mythical cultures, such as Atlantis and Lemuria. Cayce had no recollection of any of this when he awoke, though as a devout Christian the esotericism of such material made him wince when he read the transcripts.

Contrary to news coverage, Cayce was not illiterate, but neither was he well educated. Although he taught Sunday school at his Disciples of Christ church—and read through the King James Bible at least once every year—he had never made it past the eighth grade of a rural schoolhouse. While his knowledge of Scripture was encyclopedic, Cayce's reading tastes were otherwise limited. Aside from

spending a few on-and-off years in Texas, unsuccessfully trying to use his psychical abilities to
strike oil—he had hoped to raise money to open
a hospital based on his clairvoyant cures—Cayce
rarely ventured beyond the Bible Belt environs of
his childhood.

Since the tale of Jonah fleeing from the word of
God, prophets have been characterized as reluctant,
ordinary folk plucked from reasonably satisfying
lives to embark on missions that they never originally sought. In this sense, if the impending New
Age—the vast culture of Eastern, esoteric, and therapeutic spirituality that exploded on the national
scene in the 1960s and 1970s—was seeking a founding prophet, Cayce could hardly be viewed as an
unusual choice, but, historically, as a perfect one.

A Seer in Season

It was this Edgar Cayce—an everyday man, dedicated Christian, and uneasy mystic—whom New
England college student and future biographer
Thomas Sugrue encountered in 1927. When Sugrue
met Cayce, the twenty-year-old journalism student
was not someone who frequented psychics or seance
parlors. Sugrue was a dedicated Catholic who had

considered joining the priesthood. Deeply versed in world affairs and possessed of an iron determination to break into news reporting, Sugrue left his native Connecticut in 1926 for Washington and Lee University in Lexington, Virginia, which was then one of the only schools in the nation to offer a journalism degree to undergraduates. (Sugrue later switched his major to English literature, in which he earned both bachelor's and master's degrees in four years.)

As a student, Sugrue rolled his eyes at paranormal claims or talk of ESP. Yet Sugrue met a new friend at Washington and Lee who challenged his preconceptions: the psychic's eldest son, Hugh Lynn Cayce. Hugh Lynn had planned to attend Columbia but his father's clairvoyant readings directed him instead to the old-line Virginia school. (The institution counted George Washington as an early benefactor.) Sugrue grew intrigued by his new friend's stories about his father—in particular the elder Cayce's theory that one person's subconscious mind could communicate with another's. The two freshmen enjoyed sparring intellectually and soon became roommates. While still cautious, Sugrue wanted to meet the agrarian seer.

Edgar and his wife, Gertrude, meanwhile, were laying new roots about 250 miles east of Lexington in Virginia Beach, a location the readings had also selected. The psychic spent the remainder of his life in the Atlantic coastal town, delivering twice-daily readings and developing the Association for Research and Enlightenment (A.R.E.), a spiritual learning center that remains active there today.

Accompanying Hugh Lynn home in June 1927, Sugrue received a "life reading" from Cayce. In these psychological readings, Cayce was said to peer into a subject's "past life" incarnations and influences, analyze his character through astrology and other esoteric methods, and view his personal struggles and aptitudes. Cayce correctly identified the young writer's interest in the Middle East, a region from which Sugrue later issued news reports on the founding of the modern state of Israel. But it wasn't until Christmas of that year that Sugrue, upon receiving an intimate and uncannily accurate medical reading, became an all-out convert to Cayce's psychical abilities.

Sugrue went on to fulfill his aim of becoming a journalist, writing from different parts of the world for publications including the *New York Herald Tribune* and *The American Magazine*. But his life remained interwoven with Cayce's. Stricken by debilitating arthritis in the late 1930s, Sugrue sought help through Cayce's medical readings. From 1939 to 1941, the ailing Sugrue lived with the Cayce family in Virginia Beach, writing and convalescing. During these years of close access to Cayce—while struggling with painful joints and limited mobility—Sugrue completed *There Is a River*, the sole biography written of Cayce during his lifetime. When the book appeared in 1942 it brought Cayce national attention that surpassed even the earlier *Times* coverage.

Documenting the Prophet

Sugrue was not Cayce's only enthusiast within the world of American letters. *There Is a River* broke through the skeptical wall of New York publishing thanks to a reputable editor, William Sloane, of Holt, Rinehart & Winston, who experienced his own brush with the Cayce readings.

In 1940, Sloane agreed to consider the manuscript for *There Is a River*. He knew the biography was highly sympathetic, a fact that did not endear it to him. Sloane's wariness faded after Cayce's clairvoyant diagnosis helped one of the editor's children. Novelist and screenwriter Nora Ephron recounted the episode in a 1968 *New York Times* article.

"I read it," Sloane told Ephron. "Now there isn't any way to test a manuscript like this. So I did the only thing I could do." He went on:

A member of my family, one of my children, had been in great and continuing pain. We'd been to all the doctors and dentists in the area and all the tests were negative and the pain was still there. I wrote Cayce, told him my child was in pain and would be at a certain place at such-and-such a time, and enclosed a check for $25. He wrote back that there was an infection in the jaw behind a particular tooth. So I took the child to the dentist and told him to pull the tooth. The dentist refused—he said his professional ethics prevented him from pulling sound teeth. Finally, I told him he would have to pull it. One tooth more or less didn't matter, I said—I couldn't live with the child in such pain. So he pulled the tooth and the infection was there and the pain went away. I was a little shook. I'm the kind of man who believes in X-rays. About this time, a member of my staff who thought I was nuts to get involved with this took even more precautions in writing to Cayce than I did, and he sent her back facts about her own body only she could have known. So I published Sugrue's book.

Many literary journalists and historians since Sugrue have traced Cayce's life. Journalist and documentarian Sidney D. Kirkpatrick wrote the landmark record of Cayce in his 2000 biography *Edgar Cayce*. Historian K. Paul Johnson crafted a deeply balanced and meticulous scholarly analysis of Cayce with the 1998 *Edgar Cayce in Context*. And the intrepid scholar of religion Harmon Bro—who spent nine months in Cayce's company toward the end of the psychic's life—produced insightful studies of Cayce as a Christian mystic in his 1955 University of Chicago doctoral thesis (a groundbreaking work of modern scholarship on an occult subject) and later in the 1989 biography *Seer Out of Season*. While Harmon Bro died in 1997, his family has a long—and still active—literary involvement with Cayce. Bro's mother, Margueritte, was a pioneering female journalist in the first half of the twentieth century, who brought Cayce national attention in her 1943 profile in *Coronet* magazine: "Miracle Man of Virginia Beach." Bro's wife, June, and daughter, Pamela, actively teach and interpret the Cayce ideas today.

There exist many other works on Cayce—it would take several paragraphs to appreciate the best of them. But it was Sugrue, an accomplished print journalist who worked and convalesced with Cayce for several years, who fully—and this word is chosen carefully—captured Cayce's *goodness*.

Sugrue's historical Edgar Cayce is the man who grew from being an awkward, soft-voiced adolescent to a national figure who never quite knew how to manage his fame—and less so how to manage money, often forgoing or deferring his usual $20 fee for readings, leaving himself and his family in a perpetual state of financial precariousness. In a typical letter from 1940, Cayce replied to a blind laborer who asked about paying in installments: "You may take care of the [fee] any way convenient to your self—please know one is not prohibited from having a reading ... because they haven't money. If this information is of a divine source it can't be sold, if it isn't then it isn't worth any thing."

Sugrue also captured Cayce as a figure of deep Christian faith struggling to come to terms with the occult concepts that ran through his readings beginning in the early 1920s. This material extended to numerology, astrology, crystal gazing, modern prophecies, reincarnation, karma, and the story of mythical civilizations, such as Atlantis and prehistoric Egypt. People who sought readings were intrigued and emotionally impacted by this material as much as by Cayce's medical diagnoses. What's more, in readings that dealt with spiritual and esoteric topics—along with the more familiar readings that focused on holistic remedies, massage, meditation, and natural foods—there began to emerge the range of subjects that formed the parameters of therapeutic New Age spirituality in the later twentieth century.

Esoteric Philosopher

Cayce did more than assemble a catalogue of the dawning New Age. The spiritual ideas running through his readings, combined with his own intrepid study of Scripture, supplied the basis for a universal approach to religion, which, in various ways, also spread across American culture. Sugrue captures this especially well in chapter fifteen, which recounts Cayce's metaphysical explorations with an Ohio printer and Theosophist named Arthur Lammers. Cayce's collaboration with Lammers, which began in the autumn of 1923 in Selma, Alabama, marked a turn in Cayce's career from medical clair-voyant to esoteric philosopher.

Licking his wounds after his failed oil ventures, Cayce had resettled his family in Selma where he planned to resume his career as a commercial pho-tographer. He and Gertrude, who had long suffered her husband's absences and unsteady finances, enrolled their son Hugh Lynn, then sixteen, in Selma High School. The family, now including five-year-old Edgar Evans, settled into a new home and appeared headed for some measure of domestic nor-malcy. All this got upturned in September, however, when the wealthy printer Lammers arrived from Dayton. Lammers had learned of Cayce during the psychic's oil-prospecting days. He showed up at Cayce's photo studio with an intriguing proposition.

Lammers was both a hard-driving business-man and an avid seeker in Theosophy, ancient religions, and the occult. He impressed upon Cayce that the seer could use his psychical powers for more than medical diagnoses. Lammers wanted Cayce to probe the secrets of the ages: What hap-pens after death? Is there a soul? Why are we alive? Lammers yearned to understand the meaning of the pyramids, astrology, alchemy, the "Etheric World," reincarnation, and the mystery religions of ancient Egypt, Greece, and Rome. He felt certain that Cayce's readings could part the veil shrouding the ageless wisdom.

After years of stalled progress in his personal life, Cayce was enticed by this new sense of mission. Lammers urged Cayce to return with him to Dayton, where he promised to place the Cayce family in a new home and financially care for them. Cayce agreed, and uprooted Gertrude and their younger son, Edgar Evans. Hugh Lynn remained behind with friends in Selma to finish out the school term. Lammers's financial promises later proved illusive and Cayce's Dayton years, which preceded his move to Virginia Beach, turned into a period of financial despair. Nonetheless, for Cayce, if not his loved ones, Dayton also marked a stage of unprecedented discovery.

Cayce and Lammers began their explorations at a downtown hotel on October 11, 1923. In the presence of several onlookers, Lammers arranged for Cayce to enter a trance and to give the printer an astrological reading. Whatever hesitancies the waking Cayce evinced over arcane subjects vanished while he was in his trance state. Cayce expounded on the validity of astrology even as "the Source"— what Cayce called the ethereal intelligence behind his readings—alluded to misconceptions in the Western model. Toward the end of the reading, Cayce almost casually tossed off that it was Lammers's "third appearance on this [earthly] plane. He was once a monk." It was an unmistakable reference to reincarnation—just the type of insight Lammers had been seeking.

In the weeks ahead, the men continued their readings, probing into Hermetic and esoteric spirituality. From a trance state on October 18, Cayce laid out for Lammers a whole philosophy of life, dealing with karmic rebirth, man's role in the cosmic order, and the hidden meaning of existence:

> In this we see the plan of development of those individuals set upon this plane, meaning the ability (as would be manifested from the physical) to enter again into the presence of the Creator and become a full part of that creation.
>
> Insofar as this entity is concerned, this is the third appearance on this plane, and before this one, as the monk. We see glimpses in the life of the entity now as were shown in the monk, in his mode of living. The body is only the vehicle ever of that spirit and soul that waft through all times and ever remain the same.

These phrases were, for Lammers, the golden key to the mysteries: a theory of eternal recurrence, or reincarnation, which identified man's destiny as inner refinement through karmic cycles of rebirth, then reintegration with the source of Creation. This, the printer believed, was the hidden truth behind the Scriptural injunction to be "born again" so as to "enter the kingdom of Heaven."

"It opens up the door," Lammers told Cayce. "It's like finding the secret chamber of the Great Pyramid." He insisted that the doctrine that came through the readings synchronized the great wisdom traditions: "It's Hermetic, it's Pythagorean, it's Jewish, it's Christian!" Cayce himself wasn't sure what to believe. "The important thing," Lammers reassured him, "is that the basic system which runs through all the mystery traditions, whether they come from Tibet or the pyramids of Egypt, is backed up by you. It's actually the right system.... It not only agrees with the best ethics of religion and society, it is the source of them."

Lammers's enthusiasms aside, the religious ideas that emerged from Cayce's readings did articulate a compelling theology. Cayce's teachings sought to marry a Christian moral outlook with the cycles of karma and reincarnation central to

Hindu and Buddhist ways of thought, as well as the Hermetic concept of man as an extension of the Divine. Cayce's references elsewhere to the causative powers of the mind—"the spiritual is the LIFE; the mental is the BUILDER; the physical is the RESULT"—melded his cosmic philosophy with tenets of New Thought, Christian Science, and mental healing. If there was an inner philosophy unifying the world's religions, Cayce came as close as any modern person in defining it.

Cayce's "Source"

Religious traditionalists could rightly object: Just where are Cayce's "insights" coming from? Are they the product of a Higher Power or merely the overactive imagination of a religious outlier? Or, worse, are his phrases the type of muddle-fuddle produced by haunts at Ouija board sessions?

Cayce himself wrestled with these questions. His response was that all of his ideas, whatever their source, had to square with Gospel ethics in order to be judged vital and right. Cayce addressed this in a talk that he delivered in his normal waking state in Norfolk, Virginia, in February 1933, just before he turned fifty-six:

Many people ask me how I prevent undesirable influences entering into the work I do. In order to answer that question let me relate an experience I had as a child. When I was between eleven and twelve years of age I had read the Bible through three times. I have now read it fifty-six times. No doubt many people have read it more times than that, but I have tried to read it through once for each year of my life.

Well, as a child I prayed that I might be able to do something for the other fellow, to aid others in understanding themselves, and especially to aid children in their ills. I had a vision one day which convinced me that my prayer had been heard and answered.

Cayce's "vision" has been described differently by different biographers. Sugrue recounts the episode occurring when Cayce was about twelve in the woods outside his home in western Kentucky. Cayce himself places it in his bedroom at age thirteen or fourteen. One night, this adolescent boy who had spoken of childhood conversations with "hidden friends," and who hungrily read through Scripture, knelt by his bed and prayed for the ability to help others.

Just before drifting to sleep, Cayce recalled, a glorious light filled the room and a feminine apparition appeared at the foot of his bed, telling him: "Thy prayers are heard. You will have your wish. Remain faithful. Be true to yourself. Help the sick, the afflicted."

Cayce did not realize until years later what form his answered prayers would take—and even in his twenties it took him years to adjust to being a medical clairvoyant. As his new powers took shape, he labored to use Scripture as his moral vetting mechanism. Yet he consistently attributed his information to the "Source"—another subject on which he expanded at Norfolk:

As a matter of fact, there would seem to be not only one, but several sources of information that I tap when in this sleep condition.

One source is, apparently, the recording that an individual or entity makes in all its experiences through what we call time. The sum-total of the experiences of that soul is "written," so to speak, in the subconscious of that individual as well as in what is known as the Akashic records. Anyone may read these records if he can attune himself properly.

Cayce's concept of the "Akashic records" is derived from ancient Vedic writings, in which *akasha* is a kind of universal ether. This idea of universal records was popularized to Westerners in the late nineteenth century through the work of occult philosopher, world traveler, and Theosophy founder Madame H. P. Blavatsky.

A generation before Cayce, Blavatsky told of a hidden philosophy at the core of the historic faiths—and of a cosmic record bank that catalogs all human events. In Blavatsky's 1877 study of occult philosophy, *Isis Unveiled*, the Theosophist described an all-pervasive magnetic ether that "keeps an unmutilated record of all that was, that is, or ever will be." These astral records, wrote Blavatsky, preserve "a vivid picture for the eye of the seer and prophet to follow." Blavatsky equated this archival ether with the Book of Life from Revelation.

Returning to the topic in her massive 1888 study of occult history, *The Secret Doctrine*, Blavatsky depicted these etheric records in more explicitly Vedic terms (having spent several preceding years in India). In the first of her two-volume study, Blavatsky referred to "Akâsic or astral-photographs"—inching closer to the term "Akashic records" as used by Cayce.

Cayce was not the first channeler to credit the "Akashic records" as his source of data. In 1908, a retired Civil War chaplain and Church of Christ pastor named Levi H. Dowling said that he clairvoyantly channeled an alternative history of Christ in *The Aquarian Gospel of Jesus the Christ.* In Dowling's influential account, the Son of Man travels and studies throughout the religious cultures of the East before dispensing a message of universal faith that encompasses all the world's traditions. Dowling, too, attributed his insights to the "Akashic records," accessed while in a trance state in his Los Angeles living room.

Cayce, like Blavatsky, equated *akasha* with the Scriptural Book of Life. This was an example of how Cayce harmonized the exotic and unfamiliar themes of his readings with his Christian world view. In a similar vein, he reinterpreted the ninth chapter of the Gospel of John, in which Christ heals a man who had been blind from birth, to validate ideas of karma and reincarnation. When the disciples ask Christ whether it was the man's sins or those of his parents that caused his affliction, the Master replies enigmatically: "Neither hath this man sinned, nor his parents: but that the works of God should be made manifest in him" (John 9:3).

In Cayce's reasoning, since the blind man was born with his disorder, and Christ exonerates both the man and his parents, his disability must be karmic baggage from a previous incarnation. Cayce made comparable interpretations of passages from Matthew and Revelation.

In another effort to unite the poles of different traditions, Cayce elsewhere associated his esoteric search with Madame Blavatsky's. On four occasions, he reported being visited by a mysterious, turbaned spiritual master from the East—one of the *mahatmas*, or great souls, whom Blavatsky said had guided her.

The Legacy

Neither Cayce nor Sugrue lived long enough to witness the full reach of Cayce's ideas. The psychic died at age sixty-seven in Virginia Beach on January 3, 1945, less than three years after *There Is a River* first appeared. Sugrue updated the book that year. After struggling with years of illness, the biographer died at age forty-five on January 6, 1953, at the Hospital for Joint Diseases in New York.

The first popularizations of Cayce's work began to appear in 1950 with the publication of *Many*

Mansions, an enduring work on reincarnation by Gina Cerminara, a longtime Cayce devotee. But it wasn't until 1956 that Cayce's name took full flight across the culture with the appearance of the sensationally popular book *The Search for Bride Murphy* by Morey Bernstein. Sugrue's editor Sloane, having since warmed to parapsychology, published both Cerminara and Bernstein.

Bernstein was an iconic figure. A Coloradan of Jewish descent and an Ivy League–educated dealer in heavy machinery and scrap metal, he grew inspired by Cayce's career—partly through the influence of Sugrue's book—and became an amateur hypnotist. In the early 1950s, Bernstein conducted a series of experiments with a Pueblo, Colorado, housewife who, while in a hypnotic trance, appeared to regress into a past-life persona: an early-nineteenth-century Irish country girl named Bridey Murphy. The entranced homemaker spoke in an Irish brogue and recounted to Bernstein comprehensive details of her life more than a century earlier.

Suddenly, reincarnation—an ancient Vedic concept about which Americans had heard little before World War II—was the latest craze, ignited by Bernstein, an avowed admirer of Cayce, to whom the hypnotist devoted two chapters in his book.

In the following decade, California journalist Jess Stearn further ramped up interest in Cayce with his 1967 bestseller, *Edgar Cayce—The Sleeping Prophet*. With the mystic sixties in full swing and the youth culture embracing all forms of alternative or Eastern spirituality—from Zen to yoga to psychedelics—Cayce, while not explicitly tied to any of this, rode the new vogue in alternative spirituality. During this time, Hugh Lynn Cayce emerged as a formidable custodian of his father's legacy, presiding over the expansion of the Virginia Beach–based Association for Research and Enlightenment, and shepherding to market a new wave of instructional guides based on the Cayce teachings, from dream interpretation to drug-free methods of relaxation to the spiritual uses of colors, crystals, and numbers. Cayce's name became a permanent fixture on the cultural landscape.

The 1960s and 1970s also saw a new generation of channeled literature—Cayce himself originated the term *channel*—from higher intelligences, such as Seth, Ramtha, and even the figure of Christ in *A Course in Miracles*. The last was a profound and enduring lesson series, which was channeled beginning in 1965 by Columbia University research psychiatrist Helen Schucman.

A concordance of tone and values existed between Cayce's readings and *A Course in Miracles*. Cayce's devotees and the *Course*'s wide array of readers discovered that they had a lot in common; members of both cultures blended seamlessly, attending many of the same seminars, growth centers, and metaphysical churches.

Likewise, a congruence emerged between Cayce's world and followers of the twelve steps of Alcoholics Anonymous. Starting in the 1970s, twelve-steppers of various stripes became a familiar presence at Cayce conferences and events in Virginia Beach.

Cayce's universalistic religious message dovetailed with the purposefully flexible references to a Higher Power in the "Big Book," *Alcoholics Anonymous*, written in 1939. AA cofounder Bill Wilson, his wife Lois, his confidant Bob Smith, and several other early AAs were deeply versed in mystical and mediumistic teachings. Whether they viewed Cayce as an influence is unclear. But all three works—the Cayce readings, *A Course in Miracles*, and *Alcoholics Anonymous*—demonstrated a shared sense of religious liberalism, an encouragement that all individuals seek their own conception of a Higher Power, and a permeability intended to accommodate the broadest expression of religious outlooks and backgrounds.

The free-flowing tone of the therapeutic spiritual movements of the twentieth and early twenty-first centuries had a shared antecedent, if not a direct ancestry, in the Cayce readings.

Sugrue's *There Is a River* remains an irreplaceable record of Cayce's development as a spiritual messenger and pioneer. The biography captured the seer as the person who Cayce himself said he was: an ordinary man who struggled with his apparent psychical abilities and the universal religious ideas that traveled through him.

But Sugrue's biography accomplished more than just that. *There Is a River*, in its own right, became a formative document of New Age spirituality. In exploring Cayce's career, Sugrue highlighted and popularized core themes from the Cayce readings—including past-life experiences, alternative medical treatments, the imperative of the individual spiritual search, and the idea of religion as a practical source of healing.

Sugrue demonstrated how Cayce—a committed Christian, a Sunday school teacher, and, by his own reckoning, an everyday man—developed into the founding prophet of Aquarian Age spirituality. In capturing the drama and events of Cayce's journey, Sugrue elevated the clarity and endurance of the seer's message.

September 2014
New York City

(This essay originally appeared as Mitch Horowitz's introduction to *There Is a River: The Story of Edgar Cayce* by Thomas Sugrue.)

About the Author

A widely known voice of esoteric ideas, **Mitch Horowitz** is a writer-in-residence at the New York Public Library, lecturer-in-residence at the Philosophical Research Society in Los Angeles, and the PEN Award-winning author of books including *Occult America*; *One Simple Idea: How Positive Thinking Reshaped Modern Life*; and *The Miracle Club: How Thoughts Become Reality*. Mitch has written on everything from the war on witches to the secret life of Ronald Reagan for *The New York Times*, *The Wall Street Journal*, *The Washington Post*, *Salon*, Time.com, and *Politico*. *The Washington Post* says Mitch "treats esoteric ideas and movements with an even-handed intellectual studiousness that is too often lost in today's raised-voice discussions." He narrates popular audio books including *Alcoholics Anonymous* and *The Jefferson Bible*. Mitch has discussed alternative spirituality on CBS Sunday Morning, Dateline NBC, NPR's All Things Considered, CNN, and throughout the national media. The Chinese government has censored his work.